BEAU

# BLOOM

TAPLIN

Andrews McMeel
PUBLISHING

*This is your renewal.*

*This is your regrowth.*

*You may come into this softly or
bristling with thorns, beneath the light
of the sun or the moon and the stars, so
long as you always remember it is never
too late to return to the root of your
heart and begin again.*

### The Little House

Sure, things didn't work out the way
I had hoped. Maybe I thought we
would get married, have a couple
of kids, build ourselves a little house
with a fireplace in the hills, but then
what does that matter?

You are the love of my life. I
never needed us to last a lifetime to
know that.

### The First Thing

Listen, I love you. It's that clear, that
simple. And I know sometimes I can be
a disappointment, that I rarely know
what I want or think before I act,

but you should know that in half
a lifetime of spectacular messes, you
are the very first thing that's felt right.

### Fools Together

I know we needed some time apart.
Some time to reevaluate what we were
looking for. And if someday we find
our way back to each other, I know
we'll be better for it.

Still, I miss you. And most of the
time I think it would be better to be
fools together, than sensible without you.

### Espresso

I tend to be most interested in the kinds
of people who do not sweeten or dilute
themselves for the sake of people's
tastes. Who never soften the blow of
who they really are.

Like my coffee, I prefer the people
I connect with to be full-strength and
searing hot. And able to rouse my
weary, idle heart.

### September

*I can't, damn it. I can't do this,* he cried
out, shaking his head with two fingers
pressed to the bridge of his nose.

*I'm losing it. Without you, I can't
eat, I can't sleep. I look at you and all
the world unravels. Give up on you?
How? You're all I know.*

### A Defining Moment

You were an unexpected surprise, the
defining moment. The collision of stars
that slammed into me hard and sent
my neat little world plummeting into
the ocean.

I never expected it to be you, you
know? But it is you. It's all you. And
now there's no looking back.

## Peripherals

Even to this day, no matter the
time, place, or occasion, you are
always lingering in the peripherals
of my thoughts.
 Swirling and shimmering like
loose specks of dust in the light,
clouding my focus, and demanding
my attention.

## The Best Therapy

There's no therapy or medicine like
sitting alone in a secluded space
with someone you feel at home and
comfortable with.
 A little music for atmosphere
and some quality conversation and
all of your wounds and sorrows
heal themselves.

I want to be the
one whose arms
you run to whether
you have reason
to rejoice or cause
to collapse.

I can't recall a time
my heart and I were
in the same room.
I'm always a little elsewhere,
half of me here at home,
the other away with you.

## Isolation

Be aware and understanding of all people regardless of their standing and circumstances. Even the most privileged life can be miserable and isolating when the mind is sick.

We do not get to decide how happy someone should feel by how seemingly wonderful the world is around them.

### The Wrong Turn

I think you've really got to wait and
see how things play out. Sometimes a
decision you might consider a regret
or failure in the present can turn
out to be the catalyst for something
extraordinary in the end.

Some of life's wildest journeys
begin with a wrong turn.

### The Slow Death

I sense that I am slowly letting go.
That I'm growing less in love with
you every single day.

I think that's the most difficult
thing about losing someone you've
loved—the way you feel never really
dies all at once.

All you can do is wait and watch
it fade away one day at a time.

### The Chrysalis

It is as if when you love someone and
are loved in return, a chrysalis of all that
love forms around you and before long
each of you re-emerges indistinguishable
from the other—reborn as two
inseparable, symbiotic organisms with
no imagining of what life looked or felt
like before.

We relinquish control of our selves
to the us. I breathe through you. You
breathe through me. And when the bond
is broken something in each of us dies.

### Still Friends

I used to believe that the only sensible
way to cope with the end of a love was
to sever ties and move on, but I see
now that true connection is rare, and
to be understood by somebody is much
too precious a thing to lose.

So, however hard or much it hurts,
I am standing by you.

## A Good Book

Books do not dictate or teach so much
as they reveal truths you have always
carried within you.

Like a streetlamp shining on a
bare, dark road, a book only illuminates
the path; it does not create one.

That is what makes them so potent
and necessary. In an increasingly external
world, a good book is a journey inward.

## The Blueprint

I trust in the universe to unfold as it
should, to reveal my path and guide
me along on my journey.

But I also recognize that
sometimes fate requires a little push.
That while the cosmos may provide
me with the blueprint to my destiny,
it is my duty to get my hands dirty
and build something of it.

## A Meaningful Life

This is my journey and I choose to
travel alone. To devote my life to
adventure and developing passionate
connections with like-minded people.

I don't need The One to lead a
meaningful life. While some may prefer
to live under a single sun, a sky full of
stars can light the way just as well.

To hell with
happy endings
you are here
for the story.

### Sweet as a Smile

*And that's the difficult part,* she said.
*The traits you find most beautiful*
*about the people you love become the*
*things that are most painful to see after*
*they're gone.*

> *Even something as sweet as a smile*
> *can do an awful lot of damage when it*
> *comes from the person you yearn for.*

### The Liberation

Why should a relationship mean
settling down? Wait it out for someone
who won't let life escape you, who'll
challenge you and drive you toward
your dreams. Someone spontaneous
you can get lost in the world with.

A relationship, with the right
person, is a release, not a restriction.

### Spectacular Occurrences

I wish you could prepare yourself
for the spectacular occurrences in
life before they happen.

I wanted some warning. Time
to count out the number of freckles
on a face, or note the precise shade
of the sea. To immerse myself fully
in a moment before it left me.

### Walk Toward the Light

The last moments of love are an awful
lot like the end of a life. Your chest
grows tight, every memory flashes
before your eyes, and the world around
you dims and wanes as you fight
desperately to keep a dying thing alive.

But peace comes eventually. When
it does, let go. Walk toward the light.

### Whitewater River

There are certain things you'll wish
could stay the same forever, but life goes
on, with or without you, advancing
with the force of a whitewater river.

Don't exhaust energy trying to
fight the current. Instead, have a little
faith, surrender control, and trust in
the journey.

### Sudden Dread

It's starting to hurt again. Sometimes
I can go months at a time without
thinking about you. I don't like it, but
it's the only way I know how to survive.

Occasionally though it will hit me,
a terrible, hopeless dread will overcome
me, as I realize you really are gone,
maybe for good.

### Everyday Effort

Even exceptionally powerful and passionate connections require care and attention.

Chemistry might bring two people together, but it is quiet, consistent, everyday effort that makes a relationship truly remarkable.

I am little pieces
of everyone I
have met,
but I cherish
most the parts
that were yours.

### The Empath

There are certain people you meet
through life with the curious ability
to sense precisely what is stuck or
damaged in you.

They often appear unexpectedly,
with uncanny timing, and through their
aura and energy they restore your spirit
and leave the world feeling alive and
remarkable once more.

### The Softest Blue

I know you're not supposed to look
to other people to save you, but
whenever I'm around you, the world
becomes simple. My moods lift and
the skies shift from smoke and smog
to the softest blue.

I know I'm meant to save myself,
but the fact is, with you, I don't have to.

### Gravity

She was something of a contradiction,
as likely to shift the atmosphere of a
room with her charm and exuberance
as she was to blend away quietly into
a crowd unnoticed.

Beautifully warm, yet impossible
to know. She could draw you in and
hold you there like a world in the grip
of a star.

## State of Mind

Sad is something I can deal with when
I'm aware of its source. When I'm able
to take time out to develop a solution
and work my way back to a healthier
state of mind.

It is the not knowing that kills
me. The miseries unknown. A vague
air of joylessness I cannot understand,
escape, or destroy.

## Labyrinth

If we're going to talk, then let's talk.
Forget about what is polite or proper
and delve right into what is sincere and
honest. Lead me down through the
labyrinth of your true, spectacular self.

I am not interested in pleasantries.
If you want a conversation, then let's
get lost.

## Wild Conversation

I wish you'd still check in now and
again. I came to depend on our wild
conversation. The way we would
speak in depth of dead stars and
foreign cities, and share all our
innermost anxieties and aspirations.

You always left me feeling
rested and renewed, and ready to
face another day.

## On Grief

There is no right or wrong way to
grieve. Bawl until your eyes are red or
laugh like a madman in the rain. Gorge
yourself on fatty foods or take some
quiet time away. Whatever it takes to
help you cope with the loss, heal the
wound, and lead you back to a lighter
and less volatile space.

## Nurture

The most important thing you can
do for your partner is encourage and
inspire meaningful growth. Take every
opportunity to contribute to the lives
and progress of those you love.

   A sincere and positive impact will
last a lifetime, even if the relationship
does not.

## Recovery Time

The absence of someone you have loved deeply is like a weight you carry around with you wherever you go.

Though at first it may be a burden that wearies the heart, the longer you endure it and persevere, the stronger and more resilient you'll find you become.

### Irreplaceable

The most important thing you will
ever do in your life is learn to embrace
your unique, honest self. A boundless,
infinitely populated universe and there
is nothing else here quite like you.
This is your power. All those things
that make you strange and different
are what make you irreplaceable.

### The Limit of Lust

I still remember when we first met.
How wonderfully mad we were for
each other. All the passion, mayhem,
and wild adventure.

But somewhere along the way
we lost all that.

Looking back, what we called
love was just a fleeting infatuation.
A marvelous connection, but a
momentary one.

### My Finest Love

I've always believed a person's
significance to you should be measured
not by how long they last, or where
they sit on the timeline, but by how
captivating and genuine your time
with them was.

You mightn't be my final love,
but between us, you'll always be my
finest one.

### Inner Happiness

Inner happiness doesn't necessarily mean that you are free of hollow spaces or that things are always pleasant, but that no matter what happens, you trust yourself to persevere.

That you have total confidence in your capability to confront life's difficulties and ultimately overcome them.

### The Equation

Accept that not everyone will understand you, that every soul is its own equation. While you may be little more than senseless gibberish to some, others will need only a single look to get a grasp of who you are.

Never dull, dumb down, or adjust yourself to fit somewhere you don't belong.

### Cherry Blossoms

*You've changed* is an insult often intended to discourage you. Ignore it. This is your growth. Adapting and refining yourself are all necessary parts of the process.

So long as you continue to endeavour to be kind and compassionate you have nothing to be ashamed of.

I want you,
your bones,
your body heat,
the bite marks
your teeth leave,
to see how bad
and beautiful
those eyes look
beneath me.

### Drunk & Disorderly

Love does not always come into a life
loudly. It won't always come to the
door drunk and disorderly demanding
a response or reaction.

   Most of the time love is quiet and
timid, like a soft murmur in the night,
and if you're not paying close attention,
it passes you by.

## The Long Car Ride Home

The long car ride home inspires a
warmth and serenity all of its own.
The carefully curated playlists and the
spirited singalongs they encourage, the
easy, meandering conversation, and all
the soul soaring freedom of the open
road. It is like a quiet reprieve between
two worlds—a space to slow down, to
rest and recoup.

I knew well enough that soon our
time together would pass and our lives
would return to the way they were, but
for now, with my hand on the wheel,
and your hair in the wind, all that
mattered were these moments and their
magic, the stories we had shared in and
now had to tell, the sweet, gentle joy
of each other, and the feeling that all in
the world was well.

## The Tempest

Let me be clear, cross me and you
will find I can be kind and forgiving.
I've always advocated empathy and
understanding and avoid negativity
wherever I can. But wrong my friends
or family and all of my values and
virtues will be thrown to the wind.

Hurt someone I love and I
become a hurricane.

## True Identity

Immediately leave behind those who use
manipulative behavior to convince you
to change or lose your identity.

You are not putty to be played
with or a project to be perfected, but a
magnificent and unique manifestation
of the universe.

You have the right and responsibility
to be yourself.

## Faraway, Foreign Place

She never feels routine or familiar.
Whenever I see her it's like I've been
whisked away to some faraway,
foreign place.

Whether it's a few new freckles
on her cheeks, or the way her hair
hangs differently every day, I cannot
help but gaze on weakly in wonder
and astonishment.

## Grand Extravagant Gestures

A meaningful and passionate romance
isn't all about grand extravagant gestures.

In the end, it is not the restaurants,
the getaways, or expensive gifts that
are hardest to release and forget,
but the in-jokes, the long talks, your
understanding of each other. The things
you cannot replace.

On the difficult
days when the
world's on your
shoulders remember that
diamonds are made
under the weight
of mountains.

## Compromise

Yes, love is all about sacrifice and compromise, but it's also important to establish a limit.

You shouldn't have to throw your whole life away to make a relationship work.

If you have to lose yourself to please your partner, you're with the wrong person.

### Unexpected Arrival

Falling for a person isn't a process.
You can't plan for it in advance or
anticipate its arrival. Love strikes in
single moments. Anywhere. Anytime.

Someday you catch it gardening
in the sun or singing awfully in the
shower, and you think to yourself,

*Oh, I could spend all my life*
*with you.*

### The Strange Ones

I am drawn to people who embrace
their peculiarities, who aren't afraid
of drawing unwanted attention
and would never dare soften their
strangeness for others.

The kind of people who demand
their dreams into existence and speak
thoughtfully and live passionately
without reserve or reluctance.

### False God

It's a dangerous thing to romanticize
the past, to allow nostalgia to drag
up old memories from the depths
of our hearts and fashion them into
something they're not.

We built a mirage from a memory
and knelt before it like a false god.

What we called love was nothing
but foolish hope.

A memory can be a marvelous getaway, but you must never make a home there.

## Simple Pleasures

You remind me so much of life's simple pleasures and everything effortless and sweet in the world. A good read. Fresh, clean sheets. A quick dip in the sea. A cozy, rainy Sunday morning with a hot cup of coffee and no place to be.

## Inner Child

It is necessary you keep your inner child alive and well. While our adulthoods are a relentless assault of unrealistic demands and enormous responsibility, the ever-curious inner child asks the vital questions, like, *Why is this important?* and, *Will this make me happy?*

### Stargazing

We sit in silence and watch the stars,
I suppose because there are no words,
not in all the languages on earth, that
can properly describe the feeling of
being in love.

And perhaps those little burning
lights out there in the dark are the
closest we come to something that does.

### Illuminate

And never underestimate the power
of a small act of kindness. A selfless
gesture, a moment of reassurance, even
something so simple as a smile can be
enough to save a person.

After all, when you are stumbling
blind in the dark, the soft steady glow
of a single star is all that's required to
illuminate the way forward.

### Seashells

My dreaming of you is a lot like
listening to the song inside of a sea
shell. You can't see the waves or smell
the salt, but its call can make you feel
like you are right there by the ocean.

Of course, I know you're not really
here, but when you miss a thing this
badly, even the illusion is enough.

## Poor Timing

Timing is a hell of a thing. In the end, that's all it really comes down to. The potency of an attraction or the purity of a connection mean very little if you're on separate journeys.

You and I were a perfect fit, we were, there was just too much distance between us to see it.

## Saudade

They say you don't know what you've got till it's gone, but the fact is, with you, I always did.

Not a day went by I didn't thank the stars or worship the earth you walked on.

That's real loss. To know what you have, to cherish every moment, and then watch it slip away.

## The Displaced

The thing I can't stand most about myself is that I'm so rarely settled. That I cannot allow myself the space to feel satisfaction in what I have. That I avoid intimacy at all costs and court difficult things. That I dismantle everything I love because I am so terrified of ends.

Ultimately, the worst kinds of pain do not come from your enemies but the people you trust and love.

## The Contradiction

I'm such a mess of contradictions. I long for connection, but I'm unable to commit. I want love raw and honest, but would settle for a fling.

I struggle between my need for familiarity and the thirst for something new. I fall with little effort, but never find the courage to follow through.

## A Small Reminder

That's all it takes. The smallest reminder and in an instant it feels like your stomach has fallen thirty stories and collided with the steel roof of a truck.

Loss can be cruel like that, the days you think you're finally past it are the days it will punish you most.

## Malnourishment

Why does it feel like your body is shutting down every time someone dear to you walks out of your life?

Because love is a kind of nourishment, as necessary to our hearts as sustenance is to our health, and if all of a sudden it is taken away, the heart begins to consume itself.

### The Enigma

I have a tendency to become infatuated with people who are distant and difficult to understand, who share themselves sparingly, and rarely with their whole hearts.

I adore the mysteries and enigmas of people. The harder to solve, the better.

## Honeyed Words

There are those you encounter throughout your life with a unique energy all of their own. The moment of th████val is often curiously timely. And to look upon them even for a moment is to court oblivion. They█re profoundly enchanting and enigmatic, able to bend the attention of any room around them, but make no mistake, when they enter your life, it is like they have come only for you.

And like this you came to me with all the suddenness of sunlight at the dawn of a new day. To hear you voice your mind, to watch you laugh or dance, was to step for a moment out of myself and into the embrace of a dream.

In the short time we shared together you elevated my spirits, ex█████ my true heart, and restored aspects of myself I had thought I had lost. The mornings were gentler, the nights were grander, and before long I honestly thought it would be you in th█ end. I really thought it would be you there at the end of it all.

Of course, I see things clearer now. The cold truth of the matter is occasionally the greatest stories of a life are only one or two sentences long. And the people who are most capable of moving us deeply aren't always the kind to linger in love.

Instead, they wander freely from place to place, following the nature of their own fathomless hearts, enriching the lives of those fortunate enough to cross their paths through the intense, devoted passion their wild spirits inspire. They live by their own rulebook, are captivatingly themselves, and capable of making us see that we, too, are magic, and this is how they possess our hearts.

I would have loved to have fashioned a world with you, to have set aside our separate lives for something sweet and sure with each other, but as it stands, you helped me see that I have purpose and value. More than that, you helped me to see that I was always enough on my own.

Despite your absence, and all its miseries, you have left me a braver, bolder, more confident person. You, as no other could, delivered me home to myself, and that I will carry with me wherever I go.

### The Anchor

What you should look for in a partner
is someone who grounds your ego but
lifts your spirit, who moves you to
pursue your wildest dreams, but reels
you back to reality when you need it,
who applauds you on the rewards of
your successes, but never allows you
to lose sight of the reason you started.

### Matters of the Heart

When it comes to matters of the
heart, I am either overly guarded
or plummeting madly in love.
     I don't fall easily, but when
I do, it is hard and fast with a
devastating disregard for my own
safety, sanity, welfare, and health.

### A Precious Privilege

There is no more precious a privilege
than to be loved without reserve or
judgment—to look deeply into
someone's eyes and see that, despite
your many faults and flaws, you are
cherished precisely as you are.
     Once you have known a love
like that in your life, it stays with
you forever.

**Release**

Once someone has let you go
emotionally, it's over, no matter how
tightly or desperately you commit to
hang on.

Better to release yourself from
the relationship with your dignity
intact, than fight a losing battle and
risk lasting damage to your heart.

**The Best Revenge**

Truth is, the best revenge is seeking
none at all and investing that energy
in your own health and progress,
prioritizing personal goals you've
been neglecting, and working toward
creating a passionate, prosperous, and
fulfilling future of your own.

**A Soulmate**

A soulmate is a meeting of mind,
spirit, and body with someone whose
strengths, flaws, and energy perfectly
complement your own.

It is steady ground, a shelter in
a storm, a point on a map when you
are wayward and lost, the promise of
a place to come home to for as long as
you are here in the world.

### Intellect & Heart

The secret is to find someone who
engages you deeply, to form a
connection that goes further than
desire and lust.

    It's not enough to covet only
a face or a body, true chemistry
begins with the intellect and heart.

### The Choice

I've been thinking it over and what
it comes down to is this: you and I
were never going to be easy. We're
fundamentally dysfunctional, our
friends and family all disapprove, and
occasionally the fighting is so heated
you can feel it shift the temperature
of a room. Every scrap and shred
of common sense suggests we are
spectacularly, utterly wrong for each
other. And yet, in spite of all this, I
choose you.

You see, I'm not looking for
perfect or comfortable. I find you
beautiful even when you're breaking me
softly. And the very same passions that
so often lead us to conflict also fuel and
feed an unyielding need to protect
and care and sacrifice for each other.

I think the reasons we don't work
are the reasons we do. And while it may
well seem quite foolish to some, all I
want for myself in the world is your
hand and an imperfect, messy, mad life
with each other.

You see, I'm not choosing you
because our being together makes
sound, solid sense. I choose you because
you make me forget there's a choice.

Chin up, child,
in my experience,
when a life seems to
be falling to pieces,
it is usually
falling into place.

## Fealty

You're important to me. I think if there's anything that will last forever, it's that.

Whether we separate, stay in touch or rarely speak again, you will always be that little someone I really do care for, that I would sacrifice everything for to protect and keep safe.

## Sid & Nancy

I don't think I was built for a love that is comfortable or uncomplicated.

There is a restlessness in me that will always be drawn to dark, madly passionate things. The intoxicating highs and devastating lows. The chaos and the conflict.

## Childhood Homes

It is a strange thing to see you now and be unable to recall how it felt to love you. Like a half remembered dream, the essence of what we shared is there, but the details are all hazy.

Like a house I grew up in, you are still familiar to me, but the feeling of home is now missing.

## Imperishable

There are people who you will love until the end. Certain feelings are too powerful to perish and quietly survive on in the heart for life.

No matter how much we change or drift apart, in some small way, you will always be mine, and I will always be yours.

**Good Things**

It is a tough thing to let go without
any hate to hold onto. Without
betrayals of trust or irreconcilable
differences to help you break the
bonds. Dropping deadweight is easy.

It is learning when and how
to say farewell to the good things
that's hard.

There are worlds
in you, and I have
fallen in love
with every one.

**Ballads & Novels**

I had discovered, just as the ballads and novels promised, that some loves really were forever.

It was the time you had together that wasn't.

**The Road**

Never be sorry for who you are. Your personality should never be shrouded in what society expects of you.

Be shamelessly, unapologetically you. You will find the world rallies behind those who carve roads of their own.

## The Last Straw

That's it, I'm done. With you. With us.
With words that mean one thing and
actions that say another. With every
moment of dishonesty and indecision.

I see clearly now that if you
genuinely wanted to give me your time
and affection, then you wouldn't make
me beg or bleed for them.

## Spiritual Connection

No one is too good for you; it all
depends on the kind of attraction.
You can be desired for your looks or
the size of your bank account, but
when you're desired for you—your
heart, your soul, the way your mind
works—nothing else matters. Spiritual
connection surpasses all else.

## Me Time

I have discovered I am able to endure an
incredible amount of punishment and
misfortune so long as I am occasionally
allowed a few quiet moments to myself.
Some time to restore my spirit, to lick
my wounds and regroup.

A little me time and I can deal with
anything the world throws my way.

## Good Company

Befriend yourself. It is a fact of life that the people you love won't be available every moment you need them. We all lead busy lives and have our own difficulties to address.

The reality is, sometimes you'll be all you have, so you might as well enjoy the company.

## Miracles

I still believe in miracles. I want you to know that. That despite the impossible odds and all the distance between us, I still hold out a small hope that you really do come home someday.

That somehow, someway, we find each other again. And that's it. From that moment onward, I'm happy.

## Follow Through

If I give you my time and attention, you can depend on me to follow through. I'm not interested in playing games for the sake of my ego or enjoyment.

If I show an interest in you, it's because I've sensed an energy between us, and I will make every effort to explore it.

**Clarity**

One thing I am learning is that most
extraordinary things in life happen in
a moment, and if you lack the clarity
of vision to identify them when they
come, or the confidence and courage to
claim what is yours, then you miss out.


**The Stitch**

I have learned the hard way that you
can't depend on love to be more than
a stitch.

Being with someone can hold a
wound together, but you have to do
the healing yourself.

It is so
simple and
effortless with you.

Every moment
sounds like,
welcome home.

## Quality Time

The quality of a friendship should be measured by the strength of your bond and the abundance of love between you, not the number of times you catch up over coffee or go out drinking.

We all have different needs, schedules, and responsibilities. What's important is you are there when it matters.

## The Riot

I cannot be still for long. There is a riot in me all the time. A needy, restless voice in my heart endlessly urging me onward. I ache for new experiences and my hunger for adventure is boundless.

My entire life is a perpetual loop of longing for something else.

## Captivate Me

In my eyes, good conversation is the birthplace of true attraction. So open up and share with me every encounter and experience that shaped you into who you are today. Tell me all about your hopes and dreams and captivate me with your passions. Arouse my curiosity and you'll have my attention.

## Peace & Closure

Look, in this life you won't always find peace and closure. Some losses bury themselves into the heart too deeply to ever be entirely resolved or forgotten.

Sometimes the most you can really do is persevere until the pain is too small or familiar to harm you.

## Elsewhere

It's been a long time since I've felt
present with other people. Since
I've experienced moments of
genuine connection.

I'll go to parties and mingle,
and even feign interest in the
conversation, but on the inside
my heart is endlessly elsewhere.

### The Nitpick

I'm not the type to cycle in and out
of relationships. I experience true
connection rarely and would never
dare settle for less.

I would rather wait a lifetime in
isolation for something that genuinely
captivates me than rush into something
shallow or ordinary just to feel needed.

### Awfully Dull

I hope you never allow a betrayal or
bad experience to frighten you into
isolation or diminish the passions of
your heart.

Yes, love is volatile, and some
suffering is unavoidable, but a life
without it would be awfully dull.

### The Natural Order

It is the nature of all things to end
eventually. I see that now. For as long
as there's a universe, the tide will roll
in and out, cities will rise and fall, and
stars will burn and fade away.

All things have their time and we
spent ours spectacularly. That's what
matters to me.

## My Best Self

You have this extraordinary energy
about you that consumes and calms me
all at once. And the way you dismantle
my defenses and challenge me at every
turn helps me to become a stronger and
more passionate person.
　　I feel capable of anything around
you. You bring out my best self.

## Solitary Self

Listen, a rebound isn't the answer.
The solution to a broken heart isn't
finding something else to seal the
wound, but falling back in love with
your solitary self.
　　It is relearning how to enjoy
the company of your thoughts, and
trusting in your capability to navigate
a life on your own.

## Dismantle Me

You dismantle me, baby, you do.
Every lovely word that falls from
your lips gets stuck under my skin
and splinters. And when you narrow
your eyes and smile, the very core
of me cracks then crumbles.
　　I adore you, god I do, to the point
of madness, to the point of devastation.

## Snake Charmer

You enchant me. Do you understand?
I cannot resist you at all. I writhe
and dance to your every command
like a cobra captivated by a snake
charmer's spell.
    You consume me absolutely,
heart to mind, and breath to bone.
Every thought, every action, every
pulse, is yours.

## One Thousand Ships

I love senselessly or not at all. I cannot
give myself away to those who do not
consume me, no matter how kind,
committed, or honest they are.
    But capture the full attention of
my heart, and however toxic you are
for me, I would conquer the world in
your name if you asked.

I want you,
desperately,
whether we are a
match made in
heaven or a
beautiful disaster
just waiting
to happen.

## Bon Appétit

Think of your life as a dish where it is left to you to decide on the ingredients. Perhaps you would choose your aspirations as a base, overlaid with generous helpings of love and family, all seasoned lightly with just a dash of personal time set aside for your passions and hobbies.

Or perhaps what you are after is something sweeter and more decadent —spoonfuls of dark, indulgent romances, intoxicating adventure, and unforgettable experiences all blended together with only a hint of time allocated for work and other less thrilling responsibilities.

Whichever the case, the quality of your time here all depends on the care and preparation you put in, and so long as you find the end result rich and satisfying, the decision of what you create of your life is entirely up to you.

### Equal Effort

How to tell if somebody is genuinely
interested in you: if you removed all of
your effort from the equation, would
any communication remain between
you? If not, there is nothing there, and
you deserve better.

### The Boxer

There's no need to be so delicate with
your heart. It has the stamina to last
a lifetime, not a single bone to break,
and is bound securely, red with fury,
in a set of ribs built like a cage match.
    It has never required your
concern or protection. The heart
was built to take a punch.

### True Weight

If only you could immortalize the
beauty of a moment before it left you.
Embrace and memorize every minor
detail and relive precisely how it
made you feel.
    Sadly, the sweetest moments
in life usually go by unnoticed, and
rarely reveal their true weight or
worth until they are far behind you.

### A Muse and a Friend

I have found a life for me in you, I know it. Someone I could fight for and fall with, who could move me to soar further than I ever would on my own wings. I see a lover, an accomplice, a muse, and a friend.

Someone I could create something meaningful in the world with.

### An Unexpected Goodbye

Whoever said actions speak louder than words has never been silenced by the deafening howl of a small, unexpected goodbye.

### Inner Power

Oh sweet child, you are so much stronger than you know. All the power you need to survive and succeed has always been contained within you.

The only true challenge is locating the courage to rise to your feet and claim it.

## A Redefining

You completely redefine my idea of
what love is and should be. That
it needn't be possessive, volatile, or
detrimental to your well-being, but can
be selfless, gentle and consistent, and
should empower you to pursue your
passions. That it should balance and
enrich a life, not tear it to pieces.

## Fantastically Foolish

There may come a time in your life
when the universe will ask you to do
something fantastically foolish for the
person you love.

I pray that you rise to this
challenge with daring and grace. That
you always recognize the wisdom in
risking anything and everything for the
good of your heart.

## Careful Investments

Fact is, not everyone is going to like
you. There will be instances in life
where friendships cannot be forged and
you will be loathed or rejected without
reason or cause.

Let it go and move on. Some fights
just aren't worth the time or effort.
Invest your energy where it's wanted.

## Baggage

All pain you experience throughout
your life will inevitably impact you in
one way or another. You can either
allow it to impede you and stop you
dead in your tracks, or guide your path
and drive you forward.

Which it is all depends on how
you choose to carry it.

## The Performance

A funny thing happens when you miss
someone badly enough. I can be in a
room full of friendly faces, surrounded
by laughter and celebration, but to
me, it's all just light and noise. I will
smile and make small talk, but it's all
a performance.

The truth is, I'm someplace else
with you.

## Closure

Always find closure and move on
before forming new connections.
Abolish the what ifs and discard all the
baggage so you are able to approach
each relationship with a clean slate and
be safe in the knowledge that you are
able to explore its full potential with a
free and open heart.

## Words & Actions

Unfortunately, you cannot always depend on the word of others. You can have trust and faith, but ultimately you've got to wait on people to prove their sincerity and decency through their actions.

The promises of others are no more a certainty than a cloud is a guarantee of thunder.

## Anxiety

Anxiety is an urgent, deafening thing. No matter how many logical reasons you have to remain happy or positive, when it is present, you can hear nothing else.

### There You Are

Settle your heart, child. Your time will
come. One of these days you will meet
eyes with someone who makes you feel
so at home in the world you will think
to yourself, Ah, there you are.

### Unspoken

This quiet, ongoing solitude of mine is
how I say I miss you without admitting
it out loud.

### Bridges & Binds

Powerful chemistry is more than a
physical, intellectual, or even spiritual
attraction. It is an unexplainable air
of pure, unadulterated energy.
One that bridges and binds two
separate souls together. And can
reinvigorate, or dismantle, a heart
in the span of a moment.

### Yes Man

I am learning to say yes, to be daring
and spontaneous, to hurl myself into
people and places and moments without
hesitation or second-guessing myself, to
challenge my anxieties, to confront my
fears, and trust unwaveringly in chance
and fate to lead me to where I am
supposed to be.

### Beginnings

I want to begin the rest of my days with
strong cups of coffee and the sight of
your lashes fluttering open, ignoring
alarms and sharing showers, discussing
our plans and aspirations, and wishing
each other a pleasant day knowing, with
beginnings as sweet and simple as these,
it can only get better.

### The White Flag

There is something about a challenge
I find deeply attractive. I go mad
for a love that doesn't come easy.
The clashing of wits. The teasing
and toying. The want, the need, the
challenge, the conquest. When we
finally relinquish control and surrender,
I want it to taste like triumph.

## Blood & Family

You have always been a good and devoted friend to me. You speak the same language, elevate my spirits, and embrace me despite my many shortcomings and demons.

My affections for you are unyielding and true. You are family to me. And I am family to you.

### A Self Study

I am working on learning how to
be whole and free within myself, to
acknowledge my brokenness, manifest
my own happiness, and succeed and
fail gracefully.

## At Last

I still hold onto a small, childish hope
that there's someone out there in this
crazy, wild world so completely, utterly
meant for me even the stars will sigh,
*At last!* in relief at our meeting.

You're a miracle,
I still believe that,
you just happened
to someone else.

## The Contrast

What I feel for you
falls somewhere between
the unyielding
love and loyalty
of true and lifelong friends
and the deliciously dark,
indecent lust
of a heated one-night stand.

## Terms of Sale

You cannot purchase my affection with riches or a pretty face. Wealth or physical allure alone cannot satisfy the soul.

What I am looking for is an abundance of love and passion for life.

If you can incite in me a thirst to create and experience new things, a burning desire to thrive and be in the present, then you might have my heart.

## Kaleidoscopic

To me, a rich and satisfying life means one full of contrast. Give me sleep ins and soft rains, coffee shops and conversation, but also adrenaline and adventure and drunken bellows to the stars.

I am determined to embrace this extravagant life for all that it has to offer.

## The Devils

I think we have all got someone like that in our lives. Someone who gets under our skin in all those wrong and wonderful ways.

That devil who drives us mad in the night and compels us to carry out tremendous feats of foolishness.

That certain someone we adore absolutely without reason or restraint.

## Equal Partners

There is nothing quite so precious
as a productive love. One that is
respectful of your personal goals and
acknowledges all of your achievements
and triumphs.

A love where each and every
success is shared and rightfully
celebrated as a reflection of the strength
of your connection to each other.

## In the Stars

I've never known a joy more elegant
or effortless than the one I have found
with you. Our energy is infectious, the
chemistry is wild, and your crazy and
my crazy are perfectly aligned.

I am positively convinced we were
written in the stars, and if not, I will
carve our names into the sky myself.

## Good & Healthy

Let loose once in a while. Stay up too
late, drink until you drop, order the
dirtiest, fattiest, most delicious item
on the menu.

You cannot live your whole life
restricting yourself only to what is
good and healthy for the body.

Sometimes you have got to do
what is good and healthy for the soul.

*In the absence of an adequate expression of gratitude, I commit to you my self and my heart.*

*You have blessed my days with true peace and purpose. And these two pillars stand as the foundation of all that is sweet, and good, in my life.*

**So long**

Andrews McMeel Publishing
a division of Andrews McMeel Universal
1130 Walnut Street, Kansas City, Missouri 64106

www.andrewsmcmeel.com

18 19 20 21 22 SDB 10 9 8 7 6 5 4 3 2 1

ISBN: 978-1-4494-9370-7

Library of Congress Control Number: 2017949451

Written by Beau Taplin @beautaplin
Designed by Lucy Jane Brand @lucyjanebrand
Typography provided by Jenna Paige @jennapaige_art
Photography provided by Bella Kotak @bellakotak

beautaplin.com

ATTENTION: SCHOOLS AND BUSINESSES
Andrews McMeel books are available at quantity discounts with bulk purchase for educational, business, or sales promotional use. For information, please e-mail the Andrews McMeel Publishing Special Sales Department: specialsales@amuniversal.com.